CIVIC VALUES

EQUALITY UNDER THE LAW

JEANNE MARIE FORD

Cavendish Square
New York

Clifton Park- Halfmoon Public Library
475 Moe Road
Clifton Park, NY 12065

Published in 2018 by Cavendish Square Publishing, LLC
243 5th Avenue, Suite 136, New York, NY 10016

Copyright © 2018 by Cavendish Square Publishing, LLC

First Edition

No part of this publication may be reproduced, stored in a retrieval system, or transmitted in any form or by any means—electronic, mechanical, photocopying, recording, or otherwise—without the prior permission of the copyright owner. Request for permission should be addressed to Permissions, Cavendish Square Publishing, 243 5th Avenue, Suite 136, New York, NY 10016. Tel (877) 980-4450; fax (877) 980-4454.

Website: cavendishsq.com

This publication represents the opinions and views of the author based on his or her personal experience, knowledge, and research. The information in this book serves as a general guide only. The author and publisher have used their best efforts in preparing this book and disclaim liability rising directly or indirectly from the use and application of this book.

All websites were available and accurate when this book was sent to press.

Library of Congress Cataloging-in-Publication Data

Names: Ford, Jeanne Marie, 1971- author.
Title: Equality under the law / Jeanne Marie Ford.
Description: New York : Cavendish Square Publishing, [2018] | Series: Civic values | Includes index.
Identifiers: LCCN 2017029866 (print) | LCCN 2017031405 (ebook) | ISBN 9781502632081 (E-book) | ISBN 9781502631862 (pbk.) | ISBN 9781502631879 (6 pack) | ISBN 9781502631886 (library bound)
Subjects: LCSH: Equality before the law--United States. | United States. Constitution. 14th Amendment. | Discrimination--Law and legislation--United States.
Classification: LCC KF4764 (ebook) | LCC KF4764 .F65 2018 (print) | DDC 342.7308/5--dc23
LC record available at https://lccn.loc.gov/2017029866

Editorial Director: David McNamara
Editor: Kristen Susienka
Copy Editor: Rebecca Rohan
Associate Art Director: Amy Greenan
Designer: Alan Sliwinski
Production Coordinator: Karol Szymczuk
Photo Research: J8 Media

The photographs in this book are used by permission and through the courtesy of: Front cover, Rawpixel.com/Shutterstock.com; Back cover and throughout the book, Arosoft/Shutterstock.com; p. 4 Susan Law Cain/Shutterstock.com; p. 6 Maridav/Shutterstock.com; p. 7 Chris Hepburn/The Image Bank/Getty Images; p. 8 Web Gallery of Art/File: Sanzio 01 Plato Aristotle.jpg/Wikimedia Commons; p. 9 YanLev/Shutterstock.com; p. 10 Sakina Reduan/EyeEm/Getty Images; p. 12 Bildagentur-Online/UIG/Getty Images; p. 13 Print Collector/Getty Images; p. 14 U.S. Capitol/File: Declaration of Independence (1819), by John Trumbull.jpg/Wikimedia Commons; p. 18 Various/National Archives/File: Martin Luther King, Jr. I Have a Dream Speech Lincoln Memorial.jpg/Wikimedia Commons; p. 21 Bettmann Archive/Getty Images; p. 23 Sigrid Gombert/Cultura/Getty Images; p. 24 BravoKiloVideo/Shutterstock.com; p. 26 Valerii Iavtushenko/Shutterstock.com; p. 27 Matthew J. Lee/The Boston Globe/Getty Images.

Printed in the United States of America

CONTENTS

ONE What About Equality Under the Law? **5**

TWO The History of Equality Under the Law **11**

THREE Constitutional Rights and
Equality Under the Law **19**

FOUR Equality in Society Today **25**

Glossary 29

Find Out More 30

Index 31

About the Author 32

The US Declaration of Independence says that all people are created as equals.

CHAPTER ONE

WHAT ABOUT EQUALITY UNDER THE LAW?

Americans believe in liberty and justice for all. Good citizens must work together to have a free and fair society. Everyone deserves respect and kindness. Everyone deserves the chance to succeed. Treating everyone the same is called equality.

What Is Equality?

Equality is an important part of society. It is a **civic value**. That means that most people think

> "As dear unto God is the poor peasant as the mighty prince." —Plato

equality is very important. They also make sure to practice equality in their lives. In math, the numbers on each side of an equal sign must have the same value. Social equality means that all people have the same value. However, every person is unique. We have our own opinions, interests, and talents.

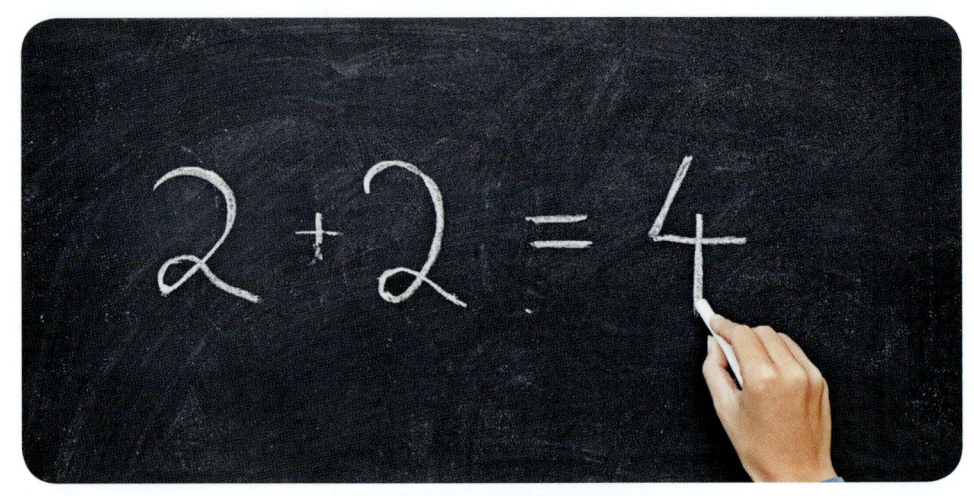

A math equation must have equal values on each side.

No matter how different we are, though, Americans have the same rights. These are called equal rights. Some examples of equal rights in the United States are the right to education and the right to marry whomever you want because you love him or her.

Justice

Justice is related to equality. It means equal treatment under the law. Many ancient societies had systems of justice. For example, Egyptian pharaohs used to hold criminal trials in dark rooms. Judges would hear only the facts. This practice helped

Lady Justice represents equality under the law.

PLATO AND ARISTOTLE

Plato (*left*) and Aristotle (*right*) taught many ideas that influenced US democracy.

Aristotle was a student of the ancient Greek **philosopher** Plato. They both taught that members of the same social class should have equal rights. Aristotle's teachings inspired many ideas in the Declaration of Independence and the US **Constitution**.

them to avoid **prejudice** toward one side. Today, US courts continue to strive for "blind justice." It shouldn't matter whether you are rich or poor, black or white, male or female. Every person should be treated equally.

In the United States, not everyone in the workplace is paid equally. In 2015, American women earned eighty cents for every dollar earned by the average working man. Women are working hard to gain equal pay in their workplaces.

Equity

Equity in the classroom helps give every student a chance to succeed.

Another form of equality is **equity**. In the classroom, it means giving everyone what they need in order to be successful. For example, a teacher may give a student with a learning disability extra time to take a test. While this student is not receiving equal treatment, he or she is being treated fairly.

What About Equality Under the Law?

In ancient Egypt, the pharaohs were wealthy and powerful rulers.

CHAPTER TWO

THE HISTORY OF EQUALITY UNDER THE LAW

Not all cultures in history treated people equally. Some of the oldest civilizations had social classes. That meant the wealthiest citizens had power over everyone else.

Equality in Ancient Societies

Other civilizations did have some kind of equality. For instance, the ancient Hebrews believed that every citizen must follow God's laws. These laws applied to all members of the Jewish community. The laws they followed were called the Ten Commandments.

Ancient Romans followed a set of laws called the Twelve Tables.

In ancient Rome, the Romans eventually agreed that the same laws should apply to everyone. They developed a set of rules called the Twelve Tables. These laws made citizens happier and society more

> "We hold these truths to be self-evident: that all men are created equal."
> —Declaration of Independence

12   Equality Under the Law

peaceful. The Twelve Tables influenced the writers of the United States Bill of Rights almost two thousand years later.

The ancient Greeks had the right to participate in making and changing laws. Their system of government was called a **democracy**. The Greeks believed that in a democracy, people should have freedom and equality.

Citizens gathered together to vote in ancient Greece.

The United States

The United States government is a democracy too. When the country became independent in 1783, the country's leaders had to come up with rules for everyone to follow. They wrote these rules down. The Declaration of Independence states some of these rules. It begins by naming Americans' most important rights. These include "life, liberty, and the pursuit of happiness." Everyone is also meant to be equal. The declaration states

Thomas Jefferson and others gathered in 1776 to present the Declaration of Independence.

Only white adult males who owned property could vote in the United States' first presidential election in 1789. About four out of five people were not allowed to participate in their own government.

Equality Under the Law

EMANCIPATION PROCLAMATION

The United States fought a war within itself from 1861 to 1865. It is called the Civil War. Some people fighting in the Civil War thought everyone should be equal. In the South, people were not equal. Many slaves lived there. During the Civil War, a document called the Emancipation Proclamation said slavery should not exist in America and all people should be equal. It would be many more years until everyone was equal, but the Emancipation Proclamation was a start.

that because people are equal, we all deserve the same rights under the law.

However, equality was not given to everyone immediately. It took many years for groups of people called **minorities** to gain full equality.

CHRONOLOGY

circa 1400 BCE Hebrew Law is established and followed in Israel.

circa 450 BCE The Twelve Tables laws are written and followed in Rome.

1776 CE The Declaration of Independence is written.

1863 The Emancipation Proclamation is issued by Abraham Lincoln.

1865 The Thirteenth Amendment is passed.

1868 The Fourteenth Amendment is passed.

1870 The Fifteenth Amendment is passed.

1919 The Nineteenth Amendment is passed.

1954 *Brown v. Board of Education of Topeka* case is decided by the Supreme Court.

1972 The Equal Rights Amendment is debated.

1990 The Americans with Disabilities Act is passed.

Dr. Martin Luther King Jr. fought for equal rights. Here, he gives his most famous speech in Washington, DC, in 1963.

CHAPTER THREE

CONSTITUTIONAL RIGHTS AND EQUALITY UNDER THE LAW

The US Constitution does not mention the word "equality." Changes, called amendments, were passed later to make sure all citizens had the same rights and were equal. These amendments are part of the US Constitution and are a part of the law today.

Amendments and Equality

After the Civil War ended in 1865, Congress passed three amendments. These gave former slaves equal rights. The Thirteenth Amendment made slavery illegal. The Fourteenth Amendment gave citizenship to every person born in the United States. Under the Fourteenth Amendment, everyone also had "equal protection of the laws." The Fifteenth Amendment gave all men the right to vote.

> "I have a dream that one day this nation will rise up and live out the true meaning of its creed: that all men are created equal." —Dr. Martin Luther King Jr., civil rights leader

However, not everyone was equal. Women could not vote until 1920, after the Nineteenth Amendment was passed. It gave all women the right to vote.

Segregation

Not everyone was treated equally after these amendments became law. Many Southern states passed new laws to keep African Americans from voting. **Segregation** laws prevented them from visiting places where only whites were allowed, such as restaurants and pools.

In the 1950s and 1960s, segregation laws promoted inequality.

   In the South, segregation also kept African American and white children from attending schools together. These states called their schools "separate but equal." However, they were not really equal. The government spent much more money on the schools attended by white students.

> In 1972, Congress passed the Equal Rights Amendment. It was supposed to guarantee that women would have the same rights as men. However, it never became law.

In 1954, the Supreme Court ruled in the *Brown v. Board of Education of Topeka* case that "separate but equal" was illegal under the Fourteenth Amendment.

ABIGAIL ADAMS

In 1776, future US president John Adams received a letter from his wife, Abigail. She wrote: "In the new code of laws [later, the Constitution], please remember the ladies and do not put too much power into the hands of the husbands." Nonetheless, American women didn't win the national right to vote until the Nineteenth Amendment was passed in 1919.

Schools and businesses were no longer allowed to **discriminate** based on the color of a person's skin.

Americans with Disabilities Act

For years, many Americans with disabilities were not allowed to go to school. Many could not work because employers refused to hire them. Many buildings lacked ramps, so people with wheelchairs could not even enter. In 1990, the Americans with Disabilities Act became law. It prevents discrimination against people with disabilities.

The Americans with Disabilities Act made it easier for people with disabilities to work and go to school.

People in the United States today have more equal opportunities than ever before, but inequality still occurs.

CHAPTER FOUR

EQUALITY IN SOCIETY TODAY

Today, women and people of color have many more opportunities than they did in the past. They can become doctors, astronauts, and soldiers. They can be Supreme Court justices or even president of the United States. Today, all citizens over the age of eighteen can vote in elections, too.

"We hold these truths to be self-evident: that all men and women are created equal."
—Elizabeth Cady Stanton, women's rights activist

Are We Equal?

Most US citizens now have equal rights under the law. However, some groups still do not have the same rights in all states.

Many people celebrate their differences and similarities in the United States with flags and other outward signs.

INCOME INEQUALITY

In the United States, the difference in income between the wealthy and the poor has been growing. This gap is called income inequality. Some people argue that the government should pass more laws to decrease income inequality. Others argue that the economy is working just as it should.

Equal rights are not the same as equal treatment. Women and minorities are more likely than others to live in poverty. They continue to face prejudice every day.

Peace and justice go hand in hand. People should always stand up for what is right.

Taking Action

All Americans must continue to work for equality. When

> In a 2015 survey, more than half of African Americans reported that they had experienced discrimination in the past month due to their race.

we see discrimination happening, we must speak out. We must always try to treat others with kindness and respect.

AFFIRMATIVE ACTION

Affirmative action laws offer opportunities to members of groups that have experienced discrimination. Some people say that affirmative action laws are no longer necessary. They argue that these laws provide an unfair advantage to some people. They say that this practice actually increases discrimination. Others argue that affirmative action is necessary to provide fair opportunities for everyone.

GLOSSARY

civic value An idea that is important to have to be a good citizen, like trust, honesty, and equality.

constitution A document that states the laws and rules of a country.

democracy A government by the people.

discriminate To treat people unfairly based on their differences.

equity Giving people what they need in order to succeed; fairness.

minority A group that does not have the most members of a population.

philosopher A person who studies many different points of view on many subjects.

prejudice An opinion about a group of people that is not based on experience.

segregation Setting people apart from one another.

FIND OUT MORE

Books

Levy, Debbie. *I Dissent: Ruth Bader Ginsburg Makes Her Mark*. New York: Simon & Schuster Books for Young Readers, 2016.

Teitelbaum, Michael. *Jackie Robinson: Champion for Equality*. New York: Sterling, 2010.

Website

Equality Under the Law?

https://learning.blogs.nytimes.com/2016/01/06/equality-under-the-law-investigating-race-and-the-justice-system/?_r=1

Video

Liberty's Kids: Born Free and Equal

https://www.youtube.com/watch?v=rkMlwKWfadY

This animated episode features the American Revolution, Abigail Adams, and the fight for civil rights.

INDEX

Page numbers in **boldface** are illustrations. Entries in **boldface** are glossary terms.

amendments, 16–17, 19–22
Americans with Disabilities Act, 17, 23
ancient Greece, 8, 13, **13**
ancient Rome, 12, **12**, 16
Bill of Rights, 13
civic value, 5
constitution, 8, 19, 22
Declaration of Independence, **4**, 8, 12, 14, **14**, 16,
democracy, 8, 13–14

discriminate, 23, 28
Emancipation Proclamation, 15–16
equal rights, 7–8, 17, 20, 22, 26–27
equity, 9
King, Dr. Martin Luther Jr., **18**, 20
minority, 15, 27
philosopher, 8, **8**
prejudice, 8, 27
right to vote, 20, 22, 25
segregation, 21
Ten Commandments, 12
Twelve Tables, 12–13, 16

ABOUT THE AUTHOR

Jeanne Marie Ford is an Emmy-winning television scriptwriter and holds an MFA in writing for children from Vermont College. She has written numerous children's books on a variety of subjects, including government and United States history. She also teaches college English. She lives in Maryland with her husband and two children.

Clifton Park-Halfmoon Library